Goodnight Time Tales

by Molly Brett

© The Medici Society Ltd, 1982   Printed in England   B67   ISBN 0 85503 067 4

SNOW TIME

When the baby rabbits Muff, Puff, and Fluff peeped out of their burrow on the day after Christmas they saw that the world was white with snow. Their father Mr Long Ears said they would not be able to visit their friends, Mr and Mrs Ginger-Nut, the squirrels, in case they got stuck in a snowdrift.

The little rabbits were very disappointed as it would be dull staying in the burrow, some of their Christmas presents were broken, they had eaten too much, gone to bed very late, and were inclined to squabble. So Mrs Long Ears suggested making a big snowman and they all set off gaily with spades and a broom, seeing the tracks of other animals as they went along – the tiny footprints of Miss Tiny Mouse, Mrs Waddle Duck's flat feet, and the large paws of Mr Badger.

Presently the rabbits reached a pond covered with ice where the woodland animals were sliding, skating, or snowballing, and they soon made a splendid snowman for all to see. "Well done young rabbits!" grunted Mr Badger and bought hot roast chestnuts for them from Fuzzy Hedgehog's little barrow.

Next moment who should arrive in a flurry of snow but Mr and Mrs Ginger-Nut on a brand new sledge. "It's our Christmas present!" they chattered and invited everyone to have a ride until the sun went down, and all the animals were soon snug at home while snowflakes drifted over a sleeping world.

PIXIE CIRCUS

The pixies living in the hedge by the wild flower field were busy rehearsing for their springtime circus after the winter, and Pipkin the elf was to walk the tightrope with his two pet butterflies. He practised every day while Fuzzy the hedgehog rehearsed juggling and other tricks and the band was busy with the music, though Old Mole was rather deaf and *would* bang his drum very loudly and – not always at the right time!

Then the Dandelion Fairy thought she should start the show by dancing on her rabbit's back and became sulky because Pipkin was to be first, so Ringmaster Tufty Tail the squirrel felt quite worried as the performance began.

Pipkin started to walk the tightrope balancing his butterflies and the audience clapped loudly, but then – into the ring dashed the Dandelion Fairy, "Watch *me* and my wonderful rabbit!" she cried racing round and round while Pipkin bravely kept his balance on the tightrope, though by now nobody was watching him.

Then Old Mole realised something was wrong – he glared at the Dandelion Fairy and grunted, "She is out of turn – conceited thing!" and gave his drum a tremendous thump...BOM! BOM! The fairy's rabbit jumped with fright and tossed off his rider who landed CRASH! right in the middle of Old Mole's drum, so he could not beat it any more because of the big hole in it.

Tufty Tail the squirrel remarked to Pipkin, "Pride goes before a fall! But *you* didn't fall off the tightrope in spite of all the fuss."

TEDDY BEARS' PARTY

Buffie the teddy bear sat in the window looking very sad. Nobody knew that today was his birthday and his owner had gone to school leaving Buffie all alone. So a tear ran down his furry face just as Robin perched on the window-sill for the crumbs left for him every day.

"Why do you look so sad?" he enquired, and, on hearing the reason, told Buffie to cheer *UP*, slide *DOWN* the drainpipe outside the window, and meet him in the wood at the end of the garden where there would be a birthday surprise for him.

Buffie enjoyed sliding down the drainpipe and hurried through the garden, crawled under the gate and reached the wood where Robin had invited *all* the bears from the neighbouring houses, big and small, old and new.

"Happy Birthday to you!" they growled and squeaked, "No one knows the date of a teddy bear's birthday so we'll have a party for us all." Each bear had brought something for a picnic and the kettle was soon boiling. Mr and Mrs Brownie Bear arrived in a toy caravan because their children could not walk so far.

Little Polar Bear was frightened of a prickly hedgehog so Tough Bear gave her a pick-a-back. Aunt Fluffy stirred fudge round in a saucepan while Tinkle Bear made toast. Greedy Uncle Growler kept helping himself to the honeypot so it served him right when a wasp buzzed round and stung him, while other teddies climbed trees like wild ones.

Then it was time to go home and all the bears sang in their growly voices,

"Nobody bakes
Birthday cakes
For a Teddy Bear,
Because we fear
It is our fate
That nobody knows the D A T E."

MOLLY BRETT

A SPELL FOR SPRING-TIME

It was spring-time in the wood after the dark winter days and all the animals living there were out to enjoy the sunshine, when they saw three little elves and a fairy peeping through the bluebells and primroses.

They were looking for a home, as the apple trees in which they lived had been cut down to make way for building houses, and this pretty wood seemed just right.

The rabbits, mice, squirrels, hedgehog, and grey badger were delighted to see them, as the four skipped around exploring their new home. "Our wood has fairies in it now," the animals told each other proudly, "We are lucky to have them as they are getting rare nowadays."

But suddenly there was a loud squeal – the smallest elf had been stung by a nettle, another was frightened by a big snail, the fairy fell into a puddle, while the third elf tore his clothes on a bramble. "We can't stay here!" cried all four, "this wood is *horrid!*"

The animals begged them not to run away, "We would dig and weed but we have no garden tools," they sighed, starting to do their best with sticks and claws. Luckily the fairy knew a few spells and recited one, then clapped her hands and in a moment the animals had all the garden tools needed, for the will to work is good magic for overcoming difficulties.

The mice cut down the nettles, two robins helped hedgehog collect dead leaves, while Old Mole grunted, "Digging is warm work," so a kind-hearted toad came to help him; but a haughty pheasant nearly lost the tip of his tail as an absent-minded rabbit clipped the grass.

Soon the fairies were helping too, pushing off snails, watering the flowers, and scolding the squirrels for throwing nut-shells about.

"Now it really is a Fairy Wood," all the animals agreed, while overhead Cuckoo sang gaily and the fairies danced to his spring-time tune.

TEDDY BEAR BAND

The five teddy bears sat on a shelf in the toyshop waiting for someone to buy them.

One day two little bears called Calico and Alpaca came in with their owners. "Nobody bought you yet?" they asked and the bears sighed, "We are too expensive and it's dull sitting here all day." "Then come to our party next Wednesday," suggested Calico, "our owners are on holiday so we are having a picnic in the buttercup field."

The bears were delighted for Wednesday was early closing day and nobody would miss them. Then the biggest bear growled, "Let's give Calico and Alpaca a surprise, we'll start a band to play at the picnic." There were toy musical instruments in the shop, and the bears started to practise when closing time came. They dressed up in the uniforms for small boys which fitted quite well though the trousers were too long.

When the party day came Calico and Alpaca and their friends waited for their guests – but nobody appeared and they began to feel cross. "The shop bears are so big and expensive that they are too proud to come to our party," they grumbled, but just then music was heard and – up marched the bears from the toyshop and soon all the teddies were dancing to their music.

After the party the bears went back to the toyshop where every Wednesday they gave a concert for the dolls and toy animals until Christmas came, then they were all sold and had children to play with ever after.

"Good morning," mewed Tabby Kitten to Glossy the guinea-pig, "why are you looking so worried today?" "It's because I've forgotten to remember that my wife Flossy and our two babies were promised a summer holiday outing, but I don't know where to take them now and they will be so disappointed," replied Glossy.

"Let's have a surprise party for all the pet animals living near," suggested Tabby. "But there is no time to send out invitations," grunted the guinea-pig sadly. "Cats are quick and can go anywhere," purred the kitten, "I'll ask the rabbits, Hector the hamster, Fanny Pigeon, Jet the black kitten, Beakie the budgie, Tom Tortoise and Puck the puppy, and we'll all bring something for the picnic." After telling Glossy what to do she set off on her errand, while the guinea-pig went home a little comforted.

Next day Flossy and the baby guinea-pigs were soon asking, "When do we start on the summer outing you promised?" "We will start at half-past two," grunted Glossy, and when the time came he led them down the footpath and so on to the common, but there was nothing to be seen except gorse and heather with the hills beyond.

"Now shut your eyes and – no peeping," ordered Glossy importantly. So Flossy and the two little guinea-pigs did as they were told, then out from the bushes came all the pets and in a moment a tablecloth was spread with such a feast and Glossy squeaked, "Now open your eyes for a lovely surprise."

It was a very merry party and afterwards there were games until it was time to go home. Glossy never told the guinea-pig family that he had nearly forgotten to organise the best summer outing they had ever had!

A TREAT FOR THE TWINS

It was the Teddy Bear Twins' birthday but Mummy and Daddy Bear said nothing about a Birthday Treat and their presents of spades and buckets were disappointing, as the twins had never seen the sea or sandcastles, so they thought these must be for gardening which they did not like.

However, after breakfast Daddy Bear said suddenly, "Hurry up twins, we're off for the day in Uncle's toy car and – guess where we are going?" The twins guessed a visit to grandma, to the ice cream stall, to the river, or the sweetshop. "All wrong," chuckled their father starting the car, as Mummy Bear hurried out with the picnic basket.

Then away they went until the little bears pricked up their ears at the sound of waves breaking on the shore, the car turned a corner and there was Teddy Bear Beach with lots of bears playing on the sand.

It was fun for the twins building castles and paddling, while Mummy Bear went to sleep after rising early, but when she woke up the twins had disappeared and Daddy Bear looked worried. "I told them not to go near the Smugglers' Cave," he growled, "there are some queer bears in there who might kidnap our twins as ship's cabin boys."

Then he peered nervously into the cave's entrance from which came rumbling sounds as the smugglers rolled barrels about. But Mummy Bear pulled him back quickly for she heard squeaks from a big lobsterpot and inside were – the twins, who had crawled in through the hole in the top.

"Just the place to keep little bears out of mischief," growled their father, "and if you are not very good you shall have another present – a big lobsterpot," and that is one thing the twins hope they won't get.

NO MUSIC FOR DANCING!

On Midsummer Eve the queen of the wild flower fairies had planned a grand Ball for her favourite dancer, Rosetta. But now there would be no music for dancing as Madame Nightingale had such a sore throat after getting wet in a thunderstorm that she could not sing a note.

None of the other birds would help for, "Fairies keep such late hours," they complained, "and as we cannot sing all night, you had better ask the owl."

But the fairies were frightened of Mr Owl. He had such a big beak and sharp claws and always looked – hungry!

However the queen was determined that Rosetta should have her party and tapped timidly on Mr Owl's front door, just as he swooped down with a poor little mouse in his claws for supper. On being ordered to let it go Mr Owl hooted crossly, "Certainly not, you fairies are always meddling – go away and mind your own business!"

"Animals in trouble *are* my business," retorted the queen and, clapping her hands she cried, "May your feathers fly away and not come back till Saturday," and at her spell all Mr Owl's feathers floated off leaving him quite bald. Dropping the mouse he hurried into his house to wait for Saturday – and his feathers.

To comfort the mouse the queen said, "I would invite you to my party, but we have no music so it is all spoilt," and she looked very sad.

"My friends and I play in a little band," squeaked the mouse and quickly introduced Señor Stagbeetle's Band, to whose gay music Rosetta and all the fairies were soon dancing until dawn. And now the band plays for all the elfin balls at the fairy queen's special request.

THE NEW POLICEMAN

Fuzzy Hedgehog felt rather lonely as he scuttled through the wood, for the other animals found him too prickly to play with, although he longed for friends and to join in all that went on around him.

Just then he saw a notice on an oak tree which said –

Nest Builders and Hole Holders are asked to a
Meeting to discuss the Dangers of Traffic on Winding Way.

Mr Owl was perched on a tree stump and began his speech to the woodland folk about the trouble traffic was causing along Winding Way. "The stage coach is always late," grumbled Mr Owl, "because Mrs Pricklepin *will* drive her slow old car in the middle of the road."

"My tail gets run over," squawked Sir Percival Pheasant glaring at Old Toad who croaked hastily, "Young Whizz the Weasel goes much too fast in that sports car of his – nearly knocked me off my tricycle!" "It's not safe for children," complained Mrs Mouse and Mrs Rabbit.

"What *we* need is a Policeman to keep order", hooted Mr Owl looking very wise , "what about *you* Fuzzy my lad? No one will risk running into *your* prickles." This was a splendid idea and Mrs Mouse made a proper policeman's helmet from a scrap of blue cloth she found on a thorn bush.

Now Fuzzy feels very important holding up the cars so that the rabbit family can get home safely with their blackberries, and telling Miss Busy Liz to hurry across with her pet snail.

As for Whizz the Weasel – Mr Mole, who keeps the garage, has told him that he will get *no more petrol* unless he does as he is told by the woodland policeman, and Fuzzy knows now that even prickles need not stop one having friends and doing a useful job.

GOING SHOPPING

Little Skippy Rabbit was looking forward to a visit to the shops because tomorrow was his birthday, and he hoped there would be a present for him on his mother's shopping list. The little shops were hidden away among twisty tree roots and other animals were popping in and out of them.

Jolly Bird Jay called at the chemist; he had a sore throat from squawking too much. Mr Bun the baker was very busy, and Mrs Thrush was trying on every hat in Miss Mole's shop.

Skippy hoped his mother would visit the toyshop or the sweetshop, but she only bought vegetables and then stopped to chat with Jiggy the squirrel, while Skippy watched Flip Flop the frog in a tangle with his pet snail. "Look!" he squeaked, "that tit is helping himself to your sausages!" and the frog only just rescued them in time.

On the way home they met their neighbour Mrs Badger pulling a bulging shopping trolley.

Skippy went to bed that evening wondering if there would be no birthday present at all, but next morning there was a beautiful little tricycle for him – a wonderful surprise!

But how had it arrived without Skippy knowing anything about it? he wanted to know. "You must thank Mrs Badger," explained his mother, "it was in *her* shopping trolley yesterday so you should not see me buying it." Now Skippy rides his tricycle to the shops and Mrs Badger has his push chair for her new baby when they all go shopping.

BADGER BROCK MAKES MERRY

Christmas was coming and Badger Brock was feeling rather lonely. He looked around his large house and wished that there were other badgers to keep him company.

Being a kind animal, however, he said to himself, "Maybe I can make it a merry Christmas for the other animals in the wood, for it has been a hard winter and their stores of food must be nearly gone."

So Badger Brock packed up plenty of goodies and set off to visit his neighbours, soon coming to a small hole out of which popped Mother Mouse with several of her children. They were delighted with his gift and asked him in to share their festivities but . . . Badger Brock was much too B I G for their hole!

Next he called on the squirrels who lived in the top of a tree. They scampered down the trunk to receive their present and invited the badger to stay with them but . . . Badger Brock could not climb trees, so he trudged on through the wood until he came to the rabbits' hole with their present.

"Thank you kindly," said Mr Rabbit, "our store cupboard is quite empty! Now won't you stay and share Christmas with us?" The badger tried to get through the front door but though he squeezed and the rabbits pulled he was just . . . too B I G.

Then Badger Brock called on Old Mole who clapped his large pink paws with pleasure and grunted, "I wish I could invite you in but you are much too B I G for my narrow underground passages." Fuzzy the hedgehog, too, begged the badger to step into his little home but again the front door among the twisty tree roots was much too small.

Sadly, Badger Brock went back to his big empty house. Suddenly he heard the birds singing carols at his door. He gladly invited them in, and explained that he was lonely. The birds were too busy to stay but a robin suggested, "Why don't *you* have a party for everybody in *your* house?"

Well! Badger had never thought of *that*, so the birds promised to pass on his invitation to all the woodland animals, while he bustled about preparing a feast and soon the guests began to arrive bringing holly, ivy and mistletoe for Christmas decorations so that Badger's home soon looked very gay indeed.

Then, amid a lot of grunting and squeaking and shuffling and scuffling, in came the squirrels and Fuzzy with a little Christmas tree, all hung with presents for kind Badger Brock who had thought about others instead of being sorry for himself.

"I was too big for *your* homes," he grunted, "but now I'm glad that *my* house is large enough for a wonderful woodland party for everybody at Christmas time."